Mother to Mentor: A Journey of Pride

OrangeBooks Publication

1st Floor, Rajhans Arcade, Mall Road, Kohka, Bhilai, Chhattisgarh 490020

Website: **www.orangebooks.in**

© Copyright, 2024, Author

All rights reserved. No part of this book may be reproduced, stored in a retrieval system, or transmitted, in any form by any means, electronic, mechanical, magnetic, optical, chemical, manual, photocopying, recording or otherwise, without the prior written consent of its writer.

First Edition, 2024

ISBN: 978-93-6554-554-8

Mother to Mentor

A JOURNEY OF PRIDE

RAGNI

OrangeBooks Publication
www.orangebooks.in

My Dearest Daughters

As I sit down to write this, I'm overwhelmed with love and pride for each of you. Being your mother has been the most incredible journey of my life, one that has taught me lessons beyond anything I could have imagined. Watching you grow into strong, compassionate, and intelligent young women fills my heart with endless joy.

I want you to know that everything I do is driven by my desire to guide and support you. Life will bring its share of challenges, but remember that you have within you the strength to overcome them all. Never be afraid to follow your dreams, stand up for what's right, and stay true to yourselves.

The bond we share is one of the greatest gifts in my life. I know I've made mistakes along the way, but please remember that this journey has been a learning experience for me too. I may not be the perfect mom, but I will always strive to be the best I can for you. No matter what, I will always be by your side. Whether you need guidance, comfort, or simply a reminder of how much you're loved, know that I will be here, cheering you on at every step.

Take life's twists and turns with grace, kindness, and courage. Above all, always remember that you are deeply loved, cherished, and capable of achieving anything you set your hearts on.

With all my love and admiration,

Mom

Disclaimer

The experiences and reflections shared in this book are my own personal journey and are not intended to represent the policies, practices, or views of any specific school or institution where I have taught or am currently teaching. While I draw upon my years of experience as an educator, the stories, anecdotes, and opinions expressed are purely my own and should not be interpreted as a reflection of my current or previous workplaces. Any resemblance to actual persons, living or dead, or real events is entirely coincidental.

Ragni is an educator and mentor with a passion for storytelling in her classroom sessions. With years of experience, guiding others through mentorship and research, she brings a unique perspective to the themes of motherhood and personal growth. Her debut memoir, *From Mother to Mentor: A Journey of Pride*, reflects her deep belief in the transformative power of nurturing relationships. When not writing or working, Ragni enjoys reading and finding new ways to ensure that every child becomes a happy and a thriving individual.

From Mother to Mentor: A Journey of Pride explores the transformation from a caregiver to a guiding force in the lives of others. In this heartfelt memoir, Ragni reflects on her journey as a teacher with motherly instincts, where relationships go beyond the classroom. Drawing from years of mentorship, she shares personal experiences, exploring the challenges and joys of guiding others to their fullest potential. With a blend of research and storytelling, Ragni highlights how the roles of mentor and mother intertwine, offering lessons on patience, resilience, and the fulfillment of helping others grow. A must-read on the power of nurturing relationships. Code 6989

Name of the book: Mother to Mentor: A Journey of Pride" genre would be "memoir."

आदित्यहृदयं पुण्यं सर्वशत्रुविनाशनम् ।

जयावहं जपेन्नित्यं अक्षयं परमं शिवम् ॥

Content

Disclaimer v

Ganpati: The True Leader 1

Topic - 1 10
   Character Development 11

Topic - 2 19
   Teaching Experiences 20

Topic - 3 23
   Impact on Students 24

Topic - 4 50
   Issues Confronting 21st-Century Education 51

Topic - 5 53
   Motherhood Insights 54

Topic - 6 57
   Educational Context 58

Topic - 7 61
   Rumor Mill 62

Topic - 8 64
   The Gilded Chariot of Dawn 65

Topic - 9 67

    Lockdown – A Blessing in Disguise for Teachers 68

Topic - 10 71

    The Story of 2 Envelopes 72

Topic - 11 75

    Treasures of the Heart: A Celebration of Silent Bonds 76

Topic - 12 78

    The Silent Weight of a Teacher's Life 79

Topic - 13 83

    Personal Reflections 84

Topic - 14 89

    Between Joy and Struggle: A Parent's Dilemma 90

Topic - 15 94

    Future Aspirations 95

Topic - 16 99

    Inspirational Elements 100

Ganpati: The True Leader

A true leader is not the one who stands in front for recognition, but the one who stands beside you in silence, especially when the weight of the world feels unbearable. They are a presence you can lean on, a constant support, who cares for your well-being not because of obligation, but out of genuine compassion. Leadership is not about titles or fleeting positions; those come and go. It's about the lasting impact, the legacy that remains long after the leader is gone—the imprint left on the hearts they've touched.

Ms. Rachna Sharma, you are that leader for me. When my path seemed uncertain and I questioned my own strength, you were there, quietly guiding me forward. You didn't offer quick fixes or empty reassurances; instead, you listened deeply, understood without asking, and showed me how to find the answers within myself. Your wisdom became my anchor during my most difficult moments.

I couldn't have done it without you. You weren't just a leader in the traditional sense; you were a mentor, a friend, a lifeline. You knew how to calm the chaos, how to make sense of my tangled thoughts when I couldn't. Even now, I often reflect on how much I learned from you—not just about work, but about life. My only regret is that you weren't with me longer. I wish we could have journeyed further together, perhaps forever.

True leaders are soulmates of the spirit. They understand your struggles without you ever having to speak a word. When I was drowning in financial strain, feeling as though the world was closing in on me, you stepped in- not with grand gestures, but with a quiet strength that made all the difference. You broke down my problems, one by one, and showed me how to manage them with clarity and grace. I used to believe that leadership had to come with a certain level of authority, that it often demanded a distance between the leader and the follower. But you redefined that for me. Who says a leader has to be hypocritical or disconnected? You were always authentic, real, and present. You weren't leading from above but from beside me. That's why I call you my Ganpati—a symbol of wisdom, resilience, and grace.

In my most challenging times, you stood beside me, not because you had to, but because that's who you are. A leader who walks with those they care for, never seeking praise, never asking for recognition. Your influence in my life is immeasurable, and your example will continue to inspire me—and many others—for years to come.

You have shown me that true leadership is a rare and sacred thing. It's not found in power or position, but in the ability to lift others, to walk with them through their darkest times. You are, and always will be, a beacon of genuine leadership, someone I aspire to emulate in all that I do. You are my Ganpati, the truest of leaders.

My Journey and Reflections on Teaching and Motherhood I often feel that God is with me, not because I pray, visit temples, or wear religious symbols, but because he has scripted a life full of rich experiences for me. This script, filled with drama and adventure, seems designed to entertain and challenge me. Sometimes, I think that the unresolved issues from my travels were given to me as tests to find solutions, which in turn shaped the rewards and lessons of my life.

My journey began in a lower-middle-class family. My earliest memory is of being introduced to my family as a small baby, nestled on my father's shoulder. This memory symbolizes the start of my life's story. From a young age, I desired to be surrounded by love and care, and this yearning guided me throughout my life.

From the time I was small, I never understood where I fit in the world. I was fragile—both in body and heart. Love was scarce in my childhood home, where I was treated more like a burden than a daughter. I grew up alone in a house full of people, constantly asking myself, Why am I here? The answer that echoed back was cold, and all too familiar.

"You're a girl," they would say, as though that explained everything. "Your purpose is simple: grow up, get married, and take care of a family. Nothing else matters."

My father was kinder, gentler. He would sit with me sometimes and listen, but even he was bound by tradition. "That's just how life is," he would tell me softly when I asked, why am I here? His words offered little comfort. They only deepened the pit of confusion and sadness in my heart.

By the time I was in the 7th grade, I was no longer just a child in the house. I had become the cook, the cleaner, and the caretaker. While other children learned and dreamed in school, I learned the rhythm of cooking, cleaning, and patching clothes. No one asked me what I wanted. No one seemed to care.

Years passed in a blur of duties, and then, as expected, the day came. They arranged my marriage. I believed that this was it—my purpose fulfilled. I had done everything right, just as they had told me. But the journey ahead was even darker than I had feared. My new life wasn't mine at all.

I felt invisible, trapped in a life that had been planned for me by others, the weight of my fate crushing me with each passing day.

But something inside me refused to stay silent.

It was during those long, suffocating days of marriage that I found my strength. The one thing that kept my spirit alive was my love for children. The instinct to nurture, to care for them, became my lifeline. Despite the darkness that shrouded my life, there was a light in the laughter of children. I could see it, even if no one else could.

Slowly, the children from nearby homes began to gather. I started teaching them—small things at first, like reading and counting. I saw myself in their eager eyes, these children who were free to dream, and I wanted to give them what I never had: a chance.

As the days passed, something extraordinary happened. The more I taught, the more I realized I was healing my own wounds. In teaching, I found a purpose far greater than the one my family had forced upon me. The girl who had been raised to believe she was worth nothing, had now found her voice.

I wasn't just teaching subjects; I was teaching courage, resilience, and the power of education. I was teaching these children that they were more than their circumstances, that they could become anything, they dreamed of. And so, a teacher was born.

My life had been filled with sorrows and pain, but it was in my darkest moments that I found my greatest strength. The joy I brought to the children was the love I had never received, and through them, I finally felt the love and purpose, I had craved for so long. I realized that being a teacher was not just my destiny—it was my salvation.

As I grew older, I became an Educator —a role that allowed me to nurture and guide children. This role mirrored the essence of motherhood, which involves enduring pain and making continuous efforts for the well-being of a child. A mother's journey is marked by selfless care, carrying the weight of emotional and physical demands, and finding worth in the silence and acceptance of her sacrifices.

When I became a mother, I faced solitude and pain but emerged stronger and more resilient. I learned to appreciate the strength within me and the importance of resilience.

Teaching is often perceived as more than just a job—it becomes a calling, a mission that aligns deeply with personal values and one's sense of purpose. Reflecting on this, I feel my journey has been guided by an inner conviction that I am meant to be a teacher. I see my students not just as learners but as individuals with stories, struggles, and triumphs. Each day, I feel the weight of responsibility to nurture, uplift, and inspire them.

In many ways, my role as a teacher is intertwined with my role as a mother. Both callings demand patience, sacrifice, and a deep well of love. The fulfillment I experience from shaping young minds echoes the joy of watching my own children grow. Each smile, each breakthrough in understanding, each moment of empathy I witness in my students feels like a validation of this path I've chosen—or, perhaps, the path that chose me.

Entering the school gate each day brings a renewed sense of excitement and hope. I strive to impact the hearts and minds of my students, understanding that teaching involves a deep commitment to their well-being. I often wonder about the balance between guiding children and allowing them to develop their own paths. While I provide emotional guidance, I question how much control is appropriate and whether I should always be the scriptwriter in their lives.

I believe that emotional guidance is crucial for a child's development, but it's equally important to let them explore and create their own narratives. Effective teaching involves setting boundaries, guiding discipline, and teaching ethical behavior while allowing children the freedom to make their own choices.

As a teacher, my goal is to maintain open communication and empathetic conversations with my students. I aim to understand their perspectives, feelings, and reactions without judgment. Demonstrating the behaviors I wish to see in my students is essential. My experiences-challenges and failures included- serve as lessons for others, helping them navigate their own journeys and fostering personal growth.

The true satisfaction of teaching comes from witnessing the genuine smiles of students—smiles that light up their faces and warm the hearts of those around them. This joy is rooted in their acceptance and love, reflecting the impact of nurturing young minds. As educators, we should focus on broadening our students' perspectives and helping them understand the potential meanings of life. Love, patience, and acceptance are central to this endeavor.

"True Leadership: Where Compassion Meets Authority"

Some leaders might view the "mother instinct" as a weakness, associating it with being overly emotional or nurturing, which can conflict with traditional views of leadership that prioritize decisiveness and authority. They may believe that strong leaders should be tough, pragmatic, and focused solely on results. Additionally, they might fear that showing too much empathy or care could undermine their authority or lead to favoritism. Some worry that a nurturing approach could be perceived as a lack of seriousness or that it might blur professional boundaries.

However, I choose to think beyond these perceptions. As a teacher with a motherly instinct, I understand that true leadership involves recognizing the diverse needs of my students. I know that my weaker students require more attention and support, while the stronger ones need guidance to stay grounded and motivated. This awareness allows me to create an environment, where every child can thrive.

In my classroom, I celebrate the uniqueness of each child. When I focus on those who struggle, I'm not just providing extra help; I'm fostering resilience and self-esteem. I teach them that it's okay to seek support and that vulnerability can be a source of strength. By doing this, I empower them to overcome their challenges and realize their potential.

At the same time, I also recognize the achievements of my stronger students. I reward their efforts in ways that keep them humble and grounded, encouraging them to use their strengths to uplift their peers. This balance cultivates a sense of community in the classroom, where collaboration and support flourish. My role is not just to teach academics but to instill values of empathy, teamwork, and perseverance.

When a woman embraces her motherly instincts, she draws upon a unique well of understanding—the pains and gains of nurturing. This energy is unlike any other in the universe; it fosters connections that inspire and uplift. It teaches the importance of compassion and resilience, qualities that are essential not only in the classroom but also in life.

I believe that effective leadership transcends conventional definitions. It's about blending nurturing with assertiveness, creating a space where every student feels valued and heard. By being authentically myself, I challenge the notion that leadership must fit a specific mold. I demonstrate that empathy, care, and strength can coexist, enriching the educational experience and making a lasting impact on the lives of my students.

Ultimately, my journey as a teacher embodies the belief that true leadership lies in the ability to understand, support, and inspire others. By embracing my motherly instincts, I cultivate a learning environment where every child can flourish, and where the bonds we create lay the foundation for their future success. I am a Leader!!! and will lead my life in the same way

Topic - 1

Character Development

The Role of the Guru in Indian Mythology

In Indian mythology, the teacher, or "Guru," occupies a sacred role, bridging the realms of ignorance and knowledge, darkness and light. Their character development is rooted in spiritual growth, selflessness, and the profound relationship with their disciples (or "Shishya"). A true teacher not only possesses knowledge but also feels a calling to share it selflessly, recognizing themselves as conduits for higher wisdom.

The journey of a Guru is one of personal transformation, spiritual enlightenment, selflessness, and a commitment to guiding others on the path of knowledge. Teachers are not just sources of wisdom—they are seen as spiritual guides who must balance their own human flaws while helping others evolve, thus constantly growing themselves. Through their trials and sacrifices, they attain a higher understanding and leave an enduring legacy of wisdom.

The Moral Dilemma of Dronacharya

But do we need to be like Dronacharya? He embodies the moral dilemmas that teachers often face. Despite his vast knowledge and dedication, Dronacharya struggled with personal desires and ambitions, particularly his favoritism towards Arjuna. This bias highlights the complexities and flaws even in a revered guru.

In stark contrast to Dronacharya's struggles, is the story of Eklavya, a young tribal boy aspiring to become a great archer. In ancient lore, Eklavya's story stands as a painful reminder of the potential lost when a teacher denies a disciple the chance to grow. Eklavya, the son of a tribal chief, was denied formal training by Dronacharya, a revered teacher, solely because of his lower caste. Despite this, Eklavya's unwavering dedication led him to master the art of archery in solitude, creating a statue of Dronacharya to serve as his silent mentor. Tragically, when he sought to prove his skills, he was forced to sacrifice his thumb as guru dakshina—a poignant testament to the sacrifices made by those denied opportunities.

Eager to learn from Dronacharya, renowned for his expertise, Eklavya faced rejection due to the social hierarchy and Dronacharya's loyalty to the Kauravas. Though denied direct instruction, Eklavya's self-learning was remarkable. He carved a statue of Dronacharya and practiced archery in its presence, demonstrating the far-reaching impact of a teacher's influence—even when indirect. When Dronacharya later discovered Eklavya's exceptional skills, unease crept over him. Instead of feeling proud, he felt threatened by Eklavya's potential as a rival to Arjuna. In a troubling request for guru dakshina, he asked for Eklavya's right thumb. Out of respect for his guru, Eklavya willingly cut off his thumb, a decision that ultimately hindered his archery skills.

Favoritism in Education

This dynamic is mirrored in classrooms worldwide, where favoritism towards high-scoring students often prevails. Teachers may show preferential treatment based on personal biases or relationships. While this may seem harmless or even beneficial for favored students, it can have significant negative consequences for the classroom environment and overall learning experience. Every student deserves equal opportunities to participate, learn, and succeed. When a teacher consistently favors certain students, it fosters feelings of neglect and injustice, among others, creating an environment ripe for resentment.

Let's Not Create Any More Eklavyas: A Call to True Leadership

It is time to shift away from systems that harm the Eklavyas of the world. Instead, let us strive to embody the wisdom and compassion of the great Gurus, particularly Guru Dattatreya—an icon of selfless knowledge-sharing and endless learning.

Guru Dattatreya: The Eternal Teacher

Dattatreya, regarded as the embodiment of the Hindu Trinity—Brahma (the Creator), Vishnu (the Preserver), and Shiva (the Destroyer)—is not only a revered teacher but also a lifelong student. His philosophy teaches that the relationship between teacher and student is reciprocal; even the most learned continue to gain wisdom from those around them, including the simplicity and profundity of nature. Dattatreya learned from everything—the earth, the wind, the animals, and the people. Each lesson imparted invaluable insights that shaped his understanding of the world and his role within it.

His life exemplifies humility and openness, elevating the very essence of leadership and teaching. Dattatreya did not place himself above others but walked alongside them, guiding and learning simultaneously. This dynamic relationship fosters a spirit of collaboration, emphasizing that true education extends beyond the confines of a classroom. It thrives in the experiences and lessons shared between individuals, regardless of their backgrounds.

The Dattatreyas of Our Age: Dr. A.P.J. Abdul Kalam

In our modern world, few figures embody this ideal more than Dr. A.P.J. Abdul Kalam, the former President of India and a visionary scientist. Much like Dattatreya, Dr. Kalam believed that learning is a lifelong process and that knowledge comes from every corner of the world—from books, people, and the simplest elements of nature. His humility and ability to connect with the youth set him apart as a mentor, inspiring millions to dream big and break free from societal limitations.

Dr. Kalam's vision of India as a developed nation wasn't solely about technological advancement; it was about empowering youth to become architects of their own destinies. He viewed every student as a future leader, capable of contributing meaningfully to society. Instead of leading from a position of authority, he inspired from a place of deep humility and shared growth. His teachings, much like Dattatreya's, didn't impose; they guided, enlightened, and nurtured the seeds of potential within each individual, encouraging them to strive for excellence and embrace their unique paths.

Bridging Generations

In today's fast-paced world, where the influence of technology often overshadows personal interactions, Dr. Kalam's approach remains relevant. He encouraged young minds to embrace innovation while being grounded in strong ethical values. His message resonates with the current generation, who grapple with issues like mental health, societal pressure, and the quest for identity in an increasingly digital landscape.

For instance, the youth of today are navigating complex challenges like climate change, social injustice, and the digital divide. Dr. Kalam's vision of fostering a sense of responsibility and service among the youth serves as a guiding light. His emphasis on "dreaming big" encourages young individuals to envision a future where they can actively participate in addressing these global challenges, fostering a sense of agency and empowerment.

The Essence of Leadership: Lessons from Dattatreya and Krishna

Dattatreya's life serves as a reminder that the essence of leadership lies in embracing differences and fostering an inclusive environment where every voice is heard and valued. The ability to unite diverse thoughts and traditions creates a rich tapestry of ideas, leading to holistic growth and development.

Krishna and Arjuna: The Teacher-Disciple Bond

Equally timeless is the relationship between Krishna and Arjuna in the Bhagavad Gita. Krishna's role as Arjuna's guide transcends mere intellectual instruction. He teaches Arjuna not just about duty but also the profound nature of life and self. Like Dattatreya, Krishna exemplifies the spiritual teacher who empowers the disciple to seek self-realization, breaking through the shackles of ignorance and doubt. This dynamic relationship illustrates that true education is about awakening the inner potential within every individual.

In a similar vein, contemporary spiritual leaders like Sadhguru Jaggi Vasudev, founder of the Isha Foundation, embody Krishna's spirit by encouraging people to look inward for answers. Sadhguru emphasizes the importance of learning from life, nature, and personal experiences, mirroring the holistic approach of Dattatreya, where the entire world becomes a source of knowledge and growth. His teachings resonate with those seeking clarity in a chaotic world, guiding them on a path toward self-awareness and fulfillment.

Much like Krishna, Sadhguru offers more than just wisdom; he provides a framework for spiritual and emotional awakening. He guides individuals on a journey toward self-discovery and liberation, showing that the ultimate role of the guru is not to impose answers but to help the disciple awaken to their own truths. By nurturing this inner exploration, Sadhguru cultivates leaders who are not only knowledgeable but also deeply connected to their purpose and the world around them.

The True Meaning of Leadership

Both Dattatreya and Krishna teach that true leadership is not about domination or control; it's about awakening greatness in others. They lead not from above but from beside us, walking shoulder to shoulder with those they guide. In today's world, where leaders often seem disconnected from the people they serve, figures like Dr. A.P.J. Abdul Kalam and Sadhguru remind us that authentic leadership is rooted in humility, wisdom, and selfless service.

No More Eklavyas

We must strive for a world where no Eklavyas are left to sacrifice their gifts due to a lack of guidance. The essence of true leadership, as embodied by Dattatreya and Krishna, is nurturing—ensuring that no potential goes unrealized and no dream unexplored. Teachers, mentors, and leaders must create environments where students and followers feel empowered to grow, learn, and challenge the status quo.

To build a future where everyone has the opportunity to flourish, we must challenge the existing barriers that hinder growth. This includes advocating for educational reforms, mentorship programs, and inclusive policies that allow all individuals to thrive, regardless of their background. By doing so, we honor the legacy of Eklavya and transform his story, from one of sacrifice to one of empowerment and inspiration.

A Call to Action

Let us all take a step toward becoming the Dattatreyas and Krishnas of today, guiding with wisdom, leading with compassion, and ensuring that no soul is left to suffer in silence. Together, we can create a world where every individual's potential is recognized and celebrated, and where the lessons of the past inspire us to forge a brighter, more inclusive future.

Embracing the Digital Age

As we navigate the complexities of the digital age, it's crucial to adapt these teachings to modern contexts. Young leaders today must not only learn from traditional wisdom but also leverage technology for social good. Initiatives like online mentorship programs, social enterprises, and digital platforms for knowledge-sharing can empower the next generation to be proactive in their learning journeys.

Furthermore, social media can serve as a powerful tool for building communities and spreading awareness about crucial issues. By encouraging young individuals to engage in meaningful dialogues and share their perspectives, we cultivate a generation that values collaboration and inclusivity.

In essence, as we honor the teachings of Dattatreya, Krishna, and contemporary leaders like Dr. Kalam and Sadhguru, we pave the way for a future where the spirit of mentorship and learning thrives, ensuring that every Eklavya can rise without sacrifice.

Teaching Experiences

When I was young, it might surprise my readers to know that I was bullied by my teachers. None of them were approachable, and I didn't like any of them. They were biased, and every day was a challenge. But despite everything, I am grateful to them because they shaped who I am today. As a teacher now, I always reach out to students who are effeminate or those who need more attention to succeed. I want to be there for the students who were like me—the ones who needed help, but never received it.

Becoming a teacher felt like a gift from the mighty goddess Saraswati, who blessed me even when I had lost hope and thought I couldn't achieve anything in life. I may not be the best teacher, but I am a teacher who stands with the students who struggle. My journey started with tutoring, then moved to an urban school, and later to an international one. It vividly reminded me of what I used to learn in my Social Studies classes—urban versus rural.

In the urban school, I became an 'Amma' to my students. I wanted to do everything for these young minds, and every day was a new experience for me. I witnessed the struggles they faced. One of my students was always late for class, and I would be upset with him for missing it every day. The students' communication skills weren't great, and they were often too shy to speak. Once, in frustration, I stopped teaching the entire class because of him. He looked at me with sadness and finally said, "I sell milk and newspapers in the morning. That's why I'm always late."

I froze, my heart breaking. Goosebumps spread across my body, and I couldn't speak. From that day, the classroom changed. We all waited for him to arrive, and we became a team. The best part of being a teacher-mother is that these children, despite their innocence, could always read the pain in my eyes. They had a way of calming me down in ways that adults never could.

One experience stands out to me. One of my students often brought 5-Star chocolates to distribute in class, even though I knew it wasn't easy for his parents to afford such luxuries. I asked him where he was getting the money from, and he replied that he asked his mom for money to buy the chocolates and share them with the class.

I explained to him that earning money isn't easy and told him how hard it is to work for it. He took it as a joke and said it couldn't be that difficult. I then challenged him to try working to find out for himself. He accepted the challenge and said, "Okay, ma'am! I will do it during my summer vacation and let you know."

As summer vacation approached, I encouraged him to help his parents and see how it feels.

When school resumed after the break, the boy, Ishwar, came to me excitedly. He told me he had worked in a fan company all summer, helping wind motors from morning till evening. He showed me his bruised hands and said, "Ma'am, now I understand how much pain parents go through to raise us." Tears welled up in my eyes as I told him how proud I was of him. He had learned the meaning of life and the importance of hard work.

Every student comes from a different background, and many face challenges that are invisible to others. As I experienced with the student who sold milk and newspapers, showing understanding and empathy can change lives. A compassionate teacher can be the reason a student feels supported and motivated to learn. That school gave me so many memories. It shaped me not only as a teacher but also as a learner and a fighter. It taught me how to survive and never give up.

Topic - 3

Impact on Students

Teaching is a profession where growth is constant. I remember my early days in the classroom—filled with idealism, hope, and perhaps a bit of naivety. I thought that if I just worked hard enough, I could change the world. But the years have tempered that belief with a deeper understanding. Change happens slowly, one student at a time. Sometimes the progress is so subtle that it goes unnoticed, but it's always there, unfolding quietly over time.

I've come to realize that teaching is not about controlling outcomes but about planting seeds. Some seeds sprout right away, while others lie dormant for years, waiting for the right conditions to grow. As a teacher, my role is to plant those seeds of curiosity, compassion, and resilience. Whether I see them bloom or not is no longer the point—knowing they are there, waiting to blossom, is actually enough.

As I reflect on my journey, I realize that my experiences as both a teacher and a mother have profoundly shaped who I am today. I have faced numerous challenges, from balancing my career with parenting responsibilities to addressing the unique needs of each student. These experiences have taught me resilience and adaptability, essential qualities that continue to guide me.

Over the years, I have received heartfelt feedback from students and parents, expressing gratitude for the positive influence I've had on their lives. Seeing former students succeed and flourish is a testament to the lasting impact of effective teaching and support.

Teacher-Student Connections

Gaandla Viveknanda

TCS Chennai

Memorable Moments

Ma'am, I really feel blessed that in my book of life journey, you are the most precious person ever. I cannot define a particular moment as memorable in my life journey I spent with you. In fact, with great joy I can say that each and every moment I spent with you is a treasured memory for me. I still remember the day we visited your home for the first time on the occasion of Vinayaka Chaturthi. You treated all of us to delicious sweet Gulab Jamun along with some snacks. Then, you gave us a tour of your home, which was beautiful, and I personally enjoyed it a lot. The day was filled with light rain, the fresh smell of the soil, a cool breeze, wet roads, small water droplets on every leaf, and a peaceful, quiet atmosphere. It was one of the most memorable experiences I've had.

Note: The only "downside" was the class you gave on the human heart—but I'm only joking!

- I'll never forget when my friend, Mr. Praveen, received the Best Student Award from you.

- One of my favorite memories is of the special weekend classes, always followed by your samosa parties.
- I often tell people: I saw you, I see you, and I will see you for the rest of my life as someone who has always been there for us, helping us whenever we were in need.
- I'll never forget when you generously paid the fee for all of us to participate in the Kung Fu certification.
- Another unforgettable moment was when you held a class outside in the middle of the field, so we could all get some vitamin D.
- I also fondly remember the first food festival at school—it was such an exciting experience!
- You even distributed exam kits to all of us before our first board examination, a gesture of kindness we deeply appreciated.
- The day you played cricket with us during the Independence Day celebration sports event was such a fun and special time.

Note: These are just a few of the many moments. There are many more.

Once again, thank you so much, ma'am, for not only being our teacher but also a mentor and a friend who shaped our lives in ways we will always cherish. Your kindness, dedication, and guidance have left a lasting impact on all of us.

Smd Zubair Hussain

Genpact

I have so many fond memories with you, and I would love to share a few that stand out the most, each woven into the fabric of my heart.

Events Under Your Guidance:

Under your leadership, we successfully organized countless events that brought our school community together. One of the most memorable was Children's Day, a celebration that transformed our usual routine into a vibrant tapestry of laughter and joy. You introduced the idea of fun activities that we had never experienced before—colorful food stalls, exciting game booths, and enticing prizes. The sheer delight on the children's faces was a testament to your vision and support. It felt incredible to work together as a team, and we thrived under your guidance, turning the event into a resounding success that we still talk about today.

Science Exhibition:

Our first-ever science exhibition was another highlight, entirely sparked by your innovative idea. I vividly recall the nervous energy that buzzed among us as we prepared our project on how blind people's senses function without sight. Many of us felt overwhelmed and unsure, but your unwavering encouragement lit a fire within us. You believed in our abilities, and through your guidance, we discovered hidden skills we never knew we had. The exhibition became a celebration of our collective growth, showcasing not just our projects, but also the bonds we formed through collaboration.

Community Lunch:

Then there was the community lunch, a beautiful initiative you devised to foster unity among us. I still remember the sparkle in your eyes when you first discussed this idea with my classmates. We eagerly planned every detail, filled with excitement. The day of the lunch was magical—each of us brought dishes from our homes, creating a mosaic of flavors and cultures. Sitting together, sharing meals and stories, we created a warm sense of belonging that strengthened our connections. It was a moment of pure joy, where we all felt like one big family.

School Magazine:

Your brilliance shone once more with the concept of our school magazine. I recall the thrill in the air when you shared this idea with us and the seniors. You inspired us to contribute our stories, poems, and artwork, igniting a spark of creativity in each student. With your encouragement, we poured our hearts into the magazine, and when we finally held the first copy in our hands, it felt like we had achieved something extraordinary together.

My Class:

You treated every student with equal care and respect, but I felt a unique bond with you. My classmates and I were always excited to assist you with events and celebrations. I treasure the camaraderie we shared, especially with my close friends—Aruna, Bhanu, Prasanna, and the boys—

Sravan, Naveen, Seenu, and Murali. During your classes, we laughed, learned, and grew together. The drama performances, quizzes, and discussions were filled with life lessons that went beyond the curriculum. You taught us the importance of giving constructive feedback and encouraged us to express ourselves, which profoundly impacted my personal growth.

Fun Moments:

The joy didn't stop in the classroom; we created countless fun memories during our free time. I fondly recall our games of charades, the laughter echoing through the halls, and the excitement of the cricket match that you organized. Those moments were a delightful escape, a reminder of the joy of learning and friendship.

When You Left:

When you left our school, it felt like a piece of our hearts had been torn away. We were all in shock and filled with sadness, unsure of why you had to go. The halls felt emptier without your presence, and we missed you terribly. One day, we decided to visit your home, and even though it was a small gathering, it was filled with warmth and nostalgia. Seeing you again brought back a flood of cherished memories. You even surprised us by visiting the school once, a moment we all treasured deeply. Your presence reminded us of the impact you had on our lives, and we were grateful for the time we spent together.

Thank you for being such an inspiring teacher and a guiding light in our lives. Your influence has left an indelible mark on our hearts, and I hope these memories bring a smile to your face, just as they do to mine. These few incidents are what gave me such a beautiful year in my school life and these memories will be forever etched in my mind.

My next journey as a teacher took me to a different school, where everything contrasted sharply with my first experience. This school shaped me into the woman I am today, instilling in me individuality, self-assurance, and strength. It prompted me to reflect on the importance of resilience and dignity in the face of challenges, both at home and in society. As a teacher, this new environment provided me with the wings to soar, and their unwavering trust in my abilities empowered me to become a more effective educator.

As I stepped into my new classroom in the urban school, a wave of anticipation washed over me. Having spent years working with students from low-income families, I had witnessed their resilience in the face of adversity. Now, I was about to embark on a different journey—one that would challenge my perceptions of privilege and hardship. Initially, I assumed that wealth would equate to an easier life for my new students. After all, they had access to resources, technology, and opportunities that many of my previous students could only dream of. However, as I got to know them, I quickly realized that their lives were far more complex than I had imagined.

Stepping into a new school as a teacher was both exhilarating and daunting. This transition marked the beginning of a new chapter filled with hopes, aspirations, and the promise of making a positive impact on students' lives. Yet, along with this excitement came unique challenges, particularly in building relationships with colleagues and integrating into the school culture.

One of the most significant challenges was establishing credibility and rapport with my colleagues. Upon arrival, I sensed a palpable camaraderie amongst the existing staff members who had worked together for years. As a new teacher I felt like an outsider, grappling with the need to prove myself while navigating personal challenges. Self-doubt crept, in as I questioned whether I would succeed in this new environment.

In my experience, the diverse backgrounds and teaching styles of my colleagues presented both opportunities and challenges. While it was refreshing to encounter different pedagogical perspectives, I also had to understand the established school culture. Each school has its own unique dynamics, traditions, and unspoken rules. I often found myself unsure of how to approach team meetings, collaborate, or even participate in social gatherings. Some teachers were open and inviting, while others were more reserved.

Despite these challenges, my experience as a new teacher taught me valuable lessons about resilience and adaptability. I learned the importance of reaching out for help and building a support network with my colleagues. Establishing connections with fellow teachers, even those who were more experienced, became crucial in overcoming feelings of isolation. By seeking mentorship and support, I gradually found my place within the school community.

Impact on Students: {notes from students}

Mangunta Meghana Sai

I wanted to express how deeply you've impacted my life, far beyond academics. You were always my favorite teacher, not only because of what you taught in class but also for the life lessons you shared. During a difficult time when I struggled to find good friends, you were there for me, offering support and encouragement. I'll never forget how you called me your " ISRO scientist" after I shared my dream of working there when I was in 7th grade.

When my JEE Mains didn't go as planned, many of my teachers at FIITJEE lost hope. They moved me to a lower section and restricted me from the advanced classes, insisting I focus on my second attempt at Mains. It was a tough time, and my parents were worried. It felt like all the hard work I'd put in over the years was slipping away.

Then, out of the blue, I received a message from you saying you were still waiting for your IITian. Those words gave me a new wave of confidence and belief in myself. With your encouragement, I improved in my second Mains attempt and eventually cleared JEE Advanced.

Now I am an IITian 😊. Thank you for everything, ma'am. Your unwavering faith in me made all the difference.

Sandip Panda

My name is Sandip Panda, and I was a student of Ragni Ma'am in Silver Oaks International School in my 7th grade in the year 2018-19. From the very first day, interactions with her did not feel like talking to a new person, her warmth made all the students in the class very comfortable and filled the classroom with a really nice feeling.

Her way of teaching wasn't always trapped within the four walls of a classroom. One of the memories I remember with her very vividly was when all of us stepped out of our classroom and into our school's football ground to study a lesson. It was something very new and different compared to the regular classes which filled all the students with excitement. Trying out things like these was that made her different from any other teacher I'd had before. This memory has caused me to remember the lesson which we studied that day, even today.

Another memory which is very close to me was when I got a chance to perform a skit with ma'am along with some of my close friends in front of a large audience. It was a fun experience to prepare and perform it for so many people.

These few incidents are what made this year in my school life so beautiful and these memories will be forever etched in my mind.

Tejas Bhat

I've been lucky to have a lot of excellent teachers at my school, but Ragni ma'am was the coolest of them all. She was enthusiastic, always energetic, and had never-ending stories and wisdom to share. One can agree that kids on the brink of becoming adolescents are some of the most challenging people to handle and guide. However, she made sure we always had a cool friend with whom we could talk to. She ensured that the entire class came together to console the person feeling low because they were changing schools the next day, as well as to celebrate together when someone had achieved something, irrespective of its size. Moreover, we, as a class, kept our close friend, Rishi, in our prayers every day during our scheduled meditation time for his speedy recovery, assuring him that he was never alone in his battle.

Never did I imagine that out of all our subjects at school, Hindi classes would be the most fun and engaging classes before we met Ragni ma'am. Whenever possible, we would enact skits, narrate stories, recite poems, and perform nukkad-naataks described in the lessons of our Hindi textbook. If the lessons were dry, then she would take the class on the lawns outside, with a reward of a few minutes of free time to play on the ground once the lesson was over.

I'm still grateful to Ragni ma'am, for ensuring that my grade 7 was filled with unique, pleasurable experiences without compromising academics.

Kavya Jain Grade 8

The most beautiful memory I remember is when you gave me the chance to participate in a speech conference with Swedish students on Christmas. You have always motivated our entire class in countless things, one of which we donated money to Akshay Patra and got ourselves featured in the newspaper. Honestly, for me, 3rd grade was the best year just because I had you as my class teacher. Whenever we used to have conflicts in our class your way of explaining and consoling each one of us was just amazing. I remember I used to cry for every small fight, and you always comforted me the best anyone could ever do. My favorite memory, which I can never forget, is that in order to make me feel happy and worth it, you had asked the entire class to make cards for me. This gesture of yours was extremely good, and I couldn't ask for anything more. Once you had asked each one of us about our wish, and you gave me the golden opportunity to tell you my three wishes, one of which you prayed for to come true, and it actually came true. I'm eternally grateful to you for it. My favorite part was when you gave other students the chance to become the MLA of the class after a fruitful discussion with me and two other kids. It felt like you were the only teacher who actually understood me in every situation, just like my own mother.

Thank you for every teaching, smile, and memory you gifted me.

Snehal Kour

Some of my memories with you Ragni ma'am is of you as our teacher in school and one of the BEST teachers I've had in my life. Our classroom lectures were made so fun by Ma'am that everyone understood everything so well! We danced, conducted workshops, etc. and made learning simpler. Ma'am is like a guide; she's always there whenever we need her! Whenever we went to field trips, ma'am sat with us and played all kinds of games! Everyone is always so comfortable around her! She's the sweetest, most humble, and most importantly, the kindest teacher ever.

Talasila Bhuvana

This happened in 7th, and I was crying because some ma'am scolded me, and I came to you crying. You were the only one who understood my situation and consoled me.

My friend used to dislike me for some reason, and she would talk to you about it. Whenever I came to talk to you, she would send me away, and talk about me. But again, you never showed any partiality or anything, even though she talked about me.

We always remember you for your kindness, I was always smiling and would be happy when you were around me. You were probably the only teacher who cares about students. I was never this comfortable with any teacher in my life.

When I was in 10th grade, whenever my friends and I went to the washroom. As I was very childish; I used to pour water on my friends in the washroom. And one day, I did that to you. At that moment, I didn't understand it was wrong. But now I regret doing it. I am really sorry for that, ma'am. You knew that I poured water on you, but then you didn't scold me, or you were never harsh or rude to me. Probably no one ever, must have done that to you,

I used to like saying bye to you after the classes were over and after we got into the buses. Most of the days, after you got into the bus, I used to say bye to you.

I always missed you and your classes. I never had this connection with any of my teachers in my life. Your classes were all fun, and you would never hurt your students. I am happy that we are your first batch in school.

You were our teacher in 7th grade, and I haven't forgotten you since then because you are a very friendly teacher and you support your students.

Whenever I cried, you would console me, telling me not to cry. You always find a way to make me happy.

Rishi

My most unforgettable memory with you is when I had fallen sick and was away for a long time from school, you had taken care of me and my classes that I had missed and motivated me, which made me successful in clearing my exams and recovering my health condition. Now I am pursuing my degree, all because of your motivation and guidance that has always given me strength in facing the challenges.

We had a very great experience doing the annual opera. Basically, I was very shy and had stage fright. During this annual opera, I opened up and was able to perform on the stage. That was an amazing experience that I had with you.

We were attached to you in the next year too, when you weren't teaching our class, we would bunk our classes to meet you in another building despite the rules against roaming in the corridors.

Himasree Penmetsa

Ragni ma'am, I never knew the versatility of the Hindi language until I met you. Till then, Hindi was just a subject for me in which all I had to do was mug up answers for the exam. But you proved that Hindi was not just a textbook subject loaded with chapters. You made us realize the vibrancy hidden in this language and changed my whole perspective towards this subject. I can never forget the efforts you made to have a no textbook, no chapter curriculum for us. You didn't want our learning to be bound by means of a textbook. And that's how a whole new idea of 'Masti ki Pathshala' sprang into being. Masti ki Pathshala showed us how fun a patshala can really be when we start loving what we are learning. We had no textbook, we wrote our own chapters and learnt everything we had to, in the liveliest way possible. You motivated us to explore and to think out of the box. I still remember composing music for the poems and choreographing a dance for them later. You always had the best energy in class, and you never gave up on us despite all our mischiefs. Our never-ending lunch break discussions were always special. The values we learnt in that short time will guide us for a lifetime.

Thank you, ma'am, for listening to us... Thank you for not giving up on us... Thank you for finding the reason for our naughtiness, for giving a channel to our craziness, for creating and empowering spaces... Thank you, ma'am, for setting us free... for letting us be what we were then.

Akanksha

Every moment whenever we were together is the best memory. You always helped me in every subject, and your teaching skills are the best. You are a little strict but the sweetest teacher I know. I remember whenever you scolded me or praised me, I always improved. I still miss every class of yours.

Anitha Reddy

You were one of the best teachers I've met till now, and I was able to share how I feel, with you and even after I was done with the seventh grade, I came to meet you because you were the best and you were there to help me with anything. I had some really great memories with you, ma'am, and you were really energetic and happy which always made our classes engaging, fun and spontaneous which also helped me understand the subject well.

~ By one of my favourite students who never forgets to mail me on my birthday

My mind fails me: I don't recall all of our memories. There was one, however, that stands out the most. Do you remember that we had to present a skit on plastic in Hindi, and our class was the only class that was asked to do the skit. So, you had held auditions for us. We all had to recite a poem. If I remember it correctly, it was "Koshish karne walo ki kabhi haar nahi hoti!" by Harivansh Rai Bachchan. For some reason that day, words were just not coming out of my mouth properly. I stammered a lot and forgot a line, and I knew that I would not get selected. I felt too many things going on at that point of time, and I just started crying standing in a corner. You had then come up to me and told me that it was okay; and there is always a next time. You had given me a chance to re-audition, but I was too scared and did not take it. Later, when kids who got selected went to practice, it made me immensely sad. I felt like I was missing out. Miraculously, you came up to me and asked me if I wanted to take part, and then it was my chance. I had no lines, but still, I could be a part of the play. I could be involved, and that gave me the confidence to participate in several things later on.

There is one more that always remains with me. I had come up to you once and told you that I felt stressed about exams coming up. You told me that the word "stress" should not exist in a child's dictionary, that nothing is important enough to bother our mind about it. You said, "Instead of saying why me, say try me." As I am a little grown up now, I realize it better now, that the true meaning of life is to live without worries and enjoy every moment wholeheartedly, having dreams that excite, people to whom you are grateful are there, being grateful for those whom you have in the present and open to those in our future. For when we are about to die, we won't remember the papers that we did not do well in the exam.

So, I want to tell you that you are an amazing philosopher. Thank you for existing for me.

The Essence of Leadership: Beyond Authority

As a teacher, I have observed that leadership is often perceived as a position of authority or power; however, its true essence transcends titles and hierarchies. Many leaders, whom I closely observe, appear to be hypocrites who wield authority merely to rule rather than to lead. They often give the impression of being open-minded but tend to dismiss others' opinions, acting in self-interest rather than for the well-being of those under their guidance. Genuine leadership embodies a set of qualities that inspire, motivate, and empower others. It involves nurturing relationships, fostering collaboration, and encouraging individuals to reach their fullest potential. In an increasingly complex and interconnected world, effective leadership is more crucial than ever.

Empathy: One of the most significant elements missing in many leaders is empathy. Understanding the emotions and perspectives of others is fundamental to effective leadership. Leaders who demonstrate empathy create an environment where individuals feel valued and understood, fostering trust and collaboration. This quality allows leaders to connect with their teams on a deeper level, addressing concerns and motivating them toward a common goal.

Integrity: Leaders who uphold ethical standards and demonstrate honesty earn the respect and loyalty of their followers. Faking integrity will never build a strong foundation for leadership; instead, it cultivates mistrust and creates a culture of non-accountability within teams.

Vision: In many educational institutions, teachers are provided with a set vision for the school, often with specific targets that they must accommodate. This leaves little room for teachers to broaden their perspectives or make changes based on their experiences. Effective leaders possess a clear vision of the future and the ability to communicate it compellingly. They inspire others by painting a picture of what is possible and rallying their teams toward achieving shared objectives. This vision acts as a guiding star, steering decisions and actions in a cohesive direction.

Inspiration: True leaders inspire others to excel by creating a motivating environment. They recognize and celebrate achievements, fostering a culture of appreciation that encourages individuals to strive for excellence. This inspiration extends beyond mere words; it is reflected in their actions and commitment to the collective mission.

Inclusivity: An inclusive leader recognizes the value of diverse perspectives and actively seeks input from team members. They create an environment where everyone feels heard and respected, fostering creativity and innovation. Inclusive leadership is particularly vital in today's globalized world, where collaboration among individuals from different backgrounds leads to richer solutions and ideas.

Palli Sunitha

One day, Ragni ma'am asked every student in the class about their goals. That's when she realized that some students were studying without having a clear goal or dream. Others knew what they wanted something but had no idea how to achieve it. And then there were those who had confused their hobbies with their goals—I was one of those girls. I loved dancing and thought of it as my goal, but I never really considered it as something that I could pursue for life.

After that conversation, she began watching closely to see if I was on the right path or not. It was during this moment of reflection that I realized I didn't actually have a goal. I loved to dance, but I had never thought of making it a part of my future. It was then that I began thinking seriously about where I wanted to go in life.

She was the kind of teacher, who would ground her students whenever they lost track of their direction or were about to stray. She planted the seeds of self-awareness and guided us when we were most uncertain.

Memories with Ragni Ma'am

Rishitha Sodasu

My First Day

I still vividly remember the first day of Hindi class, feeling a mix of excitement and fear. As I sat there, my heart raced. I had no background in Hindi, and the thought of being in a room full of students who already knew the language was intimidating.

But then, Ms. Ragni spoke, with her warm smile, she asked me to introduce myself to the class. After she learnt I had no knowledge in Hindi she assured me. "We'll support you," she said, and then turning to my classmates she encouraged them to promise their support as well. I felt a wave of relief wash over me as I realized I wasn't alone. Ragni ma'am's faith in me ignited a spark of determination.

Throughout the classes that followed, she was a constant source of encouragement. Whenever I struggled, she was there to offer guidance and reassurance. Her belief in my potential pushed me to keep trying, and slowly but surely, I began to grasp the language.

Looking back, I realize that my journey in learning Hindi was made possible because of her unwavering support and kindness. Thanks to her, I not only learned Hindi but also discovered the power of encouragement and community.

Source of Unity

One of the most cherished memories I have of Ragni ma'am is how she served as the heart of our classroom. Whenever conflicts arose, she was always the first to step in, ready to listen and understand. I remember a particular argument I had with a classmate—we both were angry, and it felt like a rift had formed between us. But Ragni ma'am approached us with her calm demeanor, inviting us both to share our sides of the story without judgment.

Her ability to listen made all the difference. She never took sides. After hearing us out, she skillfully guided us toward a resolution, reminding us that life was too short for fights and that we would never forget the friendships that we formed during our school years. It was through these moments that I realized how much she truly cared about each of us and the class as a whole.

Ragni ma'am was like the glue that held us together, especially during tough times. She fostered an environment where everyone felt valued and appreciated.

Her impact on our lives went beyond just teaching Hindi; she taught us the importance of empathy, understanding, and togetherness. She emphasized how an environment like school formed the strongest of friendships and that once we grew up and went to college, our friendships would not be the same anymore. Thanks to Ragni ma'am I have a class full of friends, whom I will always cherish and remember.

Always Empathetic

I still remember one day Ragni ma'am came up to me and asked me why I was so sad. She said that my eyes looked sad and she knew something was wrong. I didn't even realize that I was dull and upset until she noticed. She listened to my personal issues and offered advice and assured me that everything would be fine. She pays attention to every student. This is when I realized that she knows us better than we do. She was like a best friend to all of us. We trusted Ragni ma'am with all of our matters and were confident enough that she would always understand us.

Her Forgiving Nature

Whenever we made mistakes, she was the first to help us rectify them. She never remembered anyone by their past mistakes instead she encouraged us to be the better versions of ourselves. She was so willing to give everyone a second chance. When my class was in a really bad position and all the teachers were angry at our behavior. She talked to our class as a whole and helped us identify the area where we went wrong and how we could resolve the issue. At that point she was the first to look past our mistakes. It was like she held us by the hand and guided us to the right path. I aspire to be as forgiving as her.

Sohan Bal

Ragni ma'am was one of the most energetic and motivational teachers we had in our 7th grade. She always treated everyone equally and was super supportive. I still remember when she played Bruno Mars song "COUNT ON ME", whenever anyone was sad, that was really comforting. She was super approachable and everyone was comfortable sharing their problems with her. She also always reminded me to focus on my hobbies, which also play a huge role in my life. We always felt safe and secure in her warm hands. Apart from all this, she was also a great teacher and no one wanted to miss a single class of hers. I also remember the days when we went outside the class, in the green meadows to study and it felt so good. We also played kho-kho in the auditorium in one of the classes. At the end I would like to say that, the guidance and motivation we have received from her, has played a vital role in shaping me what I have become now. I will forever be grateful to her and cherish these memories.

Nipeksha

Ragini ma'am- my teacher, my mentor, my other mother- Ragini ma'am will always hold a special place in my heart for the way she took all of us under her wing. I wasn't a very bright student, but Ragini ma'am pushed me and would say "Meri bachi hai tu, tujhe kyu nahi ayega?" and to date this sentence brings the biggest smile on my face. Ma'am do you remember when I came up to you with tears in my eyes because of my grades, you just looked at me opening your hands and said "Haiii mera bacha". That moment till today brings tears in my eyes, you believed in us when everyone had given up, you were there for us when everyone left and you protected us like a lioness that protects her cubs.

Ma'am I do not think you can ever imagine the kind of effect you have on my life, you inspired me to become a better human every day, be confident, be righteous, be truthful and be selfless.

I am so grateful to have you as my mentor, you are a home and you will always be!

~आपकी विद्यार्थी

~आपकी बेटी

~आपकी निपू

Topic - 4

Issues Confronting 21st-Century Education

"Teachers today face a monumental challenge: the need to be dynamic and adaptable to a generation that is constantly bombarded with fast-paced content. These students, conditioned by reels and short videos they scroll through in seconds, demand instant engagement. It's a generation that thrives on the mantra 'I'm bored,' discarding anything that doesn't immediately captivate their attention. The classroom, once a uniform space for learning, is now a diverse ecosystem of interests, abilities, and distractions. For educators, the question becomes: How do we reach them?

In my observation, one thing remains timeless—the power of stories. No matter how complex or abstract a topic may be, if educators can weave it into a compelling narrative, they can pull even the most disinterested student back into the fold. Stories, with their emotional arcs and relatable characters, transcend the distractions of modern life. When teachers transform a lesson into a story, they unlock a kind of magic that holds attention, sparks curiosity, and fosters deep understanding. In a world of fleeting content, stories remain our most powerful tool."

"Teachers in this generation need to become modern-day illusionists, weaving a maya jaal—an intricate web of intrigue—for their students. The lesson plans must be designed like mystery boxes, where each topic is wrapped in layers of curiosity and wonder. The trick is to transform every concept into an unfolding puzzle that pulls students deeper into its world. With every clue, they should feel like they're the ones unlocking the next layer, becoming so immersed that they forget it's a lesson at all.

In this environment, the students aren't passive recipients but active participants. They're the ones who must ultimately solve the mystery, giving it a conclusion that they themselves construct. When students become co-creators in their learning, the classroom is no longer a place where they simply 'endure' education. Instead, it becomes an adventure, where they chase the story to its final reveal—one that they've helped shape. In this way, teaching becomes a blend of magic and strategy, where the illusion is not deception, but deep engagement."

Motherhood Insights

Being a mother has undoubtedly influenced the way I approach teaching. The nurturing instinct, the desire to protect and support, is central to both roles. But teaching has also made me a better mother. It has taught me the importance of allowing space for growth, of guiding without controlling, of knowing when to step in and when to let go.

I've learned that, just like my students, my own children need the freedom to fail, to make mistakes, and to learn from them. While it's tempting to shield them from the world's harsh realities, I realize that my role is to prepare them for those very challenges. It's in those moments of struggle that real learning and character-building occur—whether in the classroom or at home.

Balancing motherhood and teaching has always been both challenging and rewarding. I strive to be a learner who is demonstrating the values of empathy, patience, and perseverance. This balance has taught me the importance of compassion and nurturing. As a single parent and a teacher, I often reflect on the unique challenges and insights that come with managing these two roles. The journey of motherhood, especially as a single parent, is filled with moments of joy, struggle, and growth.

Every day in the classroom, I see echoes of my own experiences in my students. Many of them come from diverse backgrounds, facing their own challenges, much like I do at home. This understanding shapes my approach to teaching—I strive to create a nurturing environment where every child feels seen and valued. I want them to know that their struggles do not define them; rather, they can be sources of strength.

One of the most profound insights I've gained is the importance of resilience. Juggling lesson plans, grading, and parenting requires a level of adaptability that pushes me to grow every day. Just as I teach my students to embrace their failures and learn from them, I remind myself that it's okay to stumble. Each misstep is a lesson in disguise, offering me the chance to model perseverance for my children.

Additionally, I've learned the value of community, I rely heavily on the support of friends, and some of my colleagues. This network has been instrumental in helping me navigate the complexities of both parenting and teaching. I encourage my students to build their own support systems, fostering connections that will serve them throughout their lives.

The emotional connection I have with my students is enriched by my experiences as a parent. I understand the weight of their emotions, whether it's excitement over a new chapter or the stress of upcoming exams. I strive to create a safe space where they can express their feelings without fear of judgment.

Furthermore, I often share age-appropriate stories from my own life with my students, helping them relate to the lessons we discuss. I want them to see that they are not alone in their struggles and that it's okay to ask for help. This transparency fosters trust and encourages open communication, allowing them to feel comfortable sharing their own experiences.

Ultimately, my dual role as a teacher and a mother enriches both aspects of my life. The challenges I face at home inform my teaching philosophy, while my experiences in the classroom inspire my parenting. By embracing both roles, I cultivate a deeper understanding of the complexities of life and aim to pass these insights on to my students.

Educational Context

The Supportive Culture of My School: A Foundation for Intellectual Growth

The educational journey of any student is profoundly influenced by the environment in which they learn. As a burgeoning educator, I have discovered that my school's culture not only nurtures my growth but also profoundly shapes my evolution as a teacher. The supportive culture of my school, which places trust in me as a teacher, aligns seamlessly with my philosophy of encouraging intellectual curiosity and resilience in my life.

At the core of a supportive school culture is the belief in the capabilities of its members. Some of my school's leadership teams have demonstrated unwavering trust in my abilities, allowing me the freedom to experiment with various teaching methods and tailor my lessons to meet the diverse needs of my students. This autonomy not only enhances my confidence as an educator but also fuels my passion for creating a vibrant and engaging classroom environment. When teachers feel trusted, they are more likely to take risks and innovate, ultimately benefiting the students they serve.

In a culture that values intellectual growth, the emphasis is placed on collaboration and open communication. My school fosters an environment where teachers share ideas, resources, and best practices. This collaborative spirit enhances our collective teaching strategies and reinforces a sense of community among educators. Moreover, the supportive culture in my school recognizes the importance of professional development. Regular workshops and training sessions equip teachers with the latest educational tools and techniques, enabling us to continually refine our practices. This commitment to professional growth is essential, as it empowers educators to stay informed and responsive to the ever-changing landscape of education. When teachers are encouraged to grow, their enthusiasm and passion for teaching translate into the classroom, inspiring students to pursue their intellectual passions.

The impact of a supportive culture extends beyond the faculty to the students themselves. In an environment where trust and support are paramount, students feel valued and understood. They are more likely to take ownership of their learning, engage in critical thinking, and explore new ideas. This safe space fosters intellectual growth, as students are encouraged to ask questions, challenge assumptions, and develop a love for learning. My goal as a teacher is to cultivate this environment by modeling curiosity, resilience, and a growth mindset.

In conclusion, the supportive culture of my school, characterized by trust, collaboration, and a commitment to professional development, aligns perfectly with my philosophy of fostering intellectual growth.

Even if I leave the school, I am confident that I will inspire future generations to embrace the joy of learning and pursue their intellectual passions with vigor.

Topic - 7

Rumor Mill

"The staff room often operates like a rumor mill, a double-edged sword that can either undermine or uplift. It serves as a production line for gossip, where whispers and half-truths can circulate unchecked, but it can also be a sanctuary for genuine support and camaraderie. In this delicate balance lies a crucial question: Are we using this space merely to vent frustrations and return to our classrooms, burdened by the very relationships we've been discussing? Or are we striving for authentic connection and understanding?

When one teacher shares their struggles, it becomes essential for others to not only listen but to actively engage. This exchange should be rooted in empathy and solidarity, reminding each other that feeling overwhelmed is part of the journey. Simple affirmations like, 'I trust you; you can do it,' resonate deeply, reinforcing the idea that we are not alone in our challenges.

However, we must also be vigilant about the fine line between support and enabling negativity. It's easy to slip into a cycle of complaint, allowing ourselves to dwell on the difficulties rather than seeking solutions. Thus, while the staff room can be a place for necessary dialogue about our experiences, it must also encourage growth and resilience.

Ultimately, this dynamic transforms not only our professional relationships but also enriches our connections with students. By modeling healthy communication and emotional intelligence in our interactions, we empower ourselves and our students to navigate their own challenges. This approach fosters an environment of trust and collaboration, where both teachers and students can thrive together.

The Gilded Chariot of Dawn

Every Morning, as the first rays of sunlight pierce through the horizon, the world awakens with renewed life and purpose. The golden beams not only bathe the earth in warmth and glory but also carry with them a promise—a promise of hope, of growth, of a new beginning.

And alongside these life-giving rays, another kind of light surges forward: the yellow buses that race across the roads, carrying the young minds of tomorrow and the warriors who teach them. These buses, like modern-day chariots, bear the weight of a mission just as sacred as the rising sun. With each stop, they gather the next generation of thinkers, dreamers, and leaders. Inside, teachers—guardians of knowledge—prepare their charges for the battles that lie ahead, not with swords or shields, but with wisdom and resilience. It feels as if two forces, the sun and these buses, march in tandem. One lights the world from above, while the other propels humanity forward from within.

As the chariots of old turned to buses, their purpose remains unchanged: to arm the young with the tools they need to face the wars of tomorrow's life. And as the buses rumble down the streets, it is not just a journey from home to school; it is a ride toward shaping the future—toward forging warriors who will fight the battles of knowledge, justice, and progress.

"Surviving the Shift: A Journey Through Virtual Learning

COVID-19 was a challenging time for me, a period marked by a battle between my need to survive and my emotional struggles. It felt like a constant war between my mind and heart, but in the end, the survival of my family was what mattered most.

When the pandemic hit, everything changed overnight. All of the home tuitions I had been providing suddenly stopped, leaving me to rely solely on my school salary. The uncertainty was overwhelming. I was willing to work around the clock, ready to do whatever it took to support my family, but willingness alone wasn't enough—the path forward was unclear.

Then, a ray of hope appeared in the form of online, virtual classes. It wasn't just a new teaching method; it was a lifeline. This transition marked the beginning of a new journey into the world of cognitive learning. With the shift to virtual education, I found myself connecting with students from across the world. It opened doors I never imagined, and even in the midst of the pandemic, I was able to continue doing what I love—teaching, guiding, and nurturing young minds, no matter the distance.

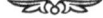

Lockdown – A Blessing in Disguise for Teachers

The COVID-19 lockdown brought with it many challenges, but as a single parent, the financial strain was overwhelming. Balancing the responsibilities of being both a sole caregiver and the primary breadwinner, the lockdown upended my already fragile financial situation.

First, the sudden closure of tuition centers severely limited my ability to work and earn an income. With no second income to rely on, the uncertainty of job security created a constant sense of financial instability. The loss of consistent income forced me to dip into my savings to cover basic needs like groceries, rent, and utilities, quickly depleting the financial cushion that I had built.

The increased cost of living during the lockdown added further strain. With children at home full-time, household expenses such as food, electricity, and internet bills skyrocketed. In conclusion, the lockdown broke me financially by reducing my income opportunities, increasing my expenses, and leaving me with no fallback. It exposed the vulnerability in such uncertain times, forcing me to rethink and rebuild my financial strategy from scratch.

"I was working as a charity volunteer through my school, but my own house didn't have food to eat. Every day, I saw the families we were helping receive essentials, and I couldn't help but feel a deep sense of irony. Here I was, distributing food to those in need, yet I was silently struggling to keep my own household afloat. Seeing others receive those items, I used to pray to the Lord, wishing I could receive them too. I felt ashamed to ask for help, not wanting my situation to overshadow the people I was trying to support.

One day, one of my students' parents, Mona, approached me. She had always been warm, but this time there was something different in the way she spoke to me—there was a quiet understanding. Knowing I was alone, she told me her husband had ordered some groceries, and she had ordered some for me as well. I was caught off guard, feeling a mix of gratitude and embarrassment. I said yes and told her I would pay her back, though deep down I knew I couldn't. I never did pay her back, and somewhere deep down, Mona knew I needed that help. She didn't make me feel small or inadequate, but instead, she offered her kindness with no strings attached.

That simple gesture from Mona became a turning point. The first online class I ever taught was offered to me by her as well. She introduced me to her circle, trusted me with her child's education, and recommended me to other parents. From there, my journey into "Cognitive Learning" an online technology platform began. What started as a small favor turned into a pathway to financial independence and personal growth. I learned not only to be grateful for the support I received but also to embrace new opportunities that came my way. It was as if Mona's kindness had unlocked a new chapter in my life, where I began to rebuild both my confidence and my livelihood.

Looking back, I realize how pivotal those moments were. The hardships I faced during that time pushed me to grow in ways I never imagined. And while the road wasn't easy, Mona's unexpected generosity became the stepping stone that led me to a career in education that I now cherish."

The lockdown also highlighted the resilience and adaptability of teachers. Faced with unprecedented challenges, teachers found themselves thrust into new roles, learning new skills, and adapting to digital platforms overnight. Despite the hardships, the lockdown opened doors for educators, pushing them out of their comfort zones and leading to growth, innovation, and collaboration in ways that might not have been possible otherwise. As schools returned to normalcy, the lessons learned during this period will continue to shape education for years to come, proving that, indeed, lockdown was a blessing in disguise for teachers.

Topic - 10

The Story of 2 Envelopes

Leaving an emotionally overwhelming and stressful marriage may be the best way to move forward, but the reality is far from easy. In a society that often condemns rather than supports, separation becomes a labyrinth of guilt and fear. "The ego complicates things further by playing all sorts of games, were bruised from years of being ignored, and played tricks on me, blurring the lines between love and failure. "On my birthday, I received a life-changing envelope. When I tore it open, it felt as though the earth cracked beneath my feet—it was a divorce letter from my husband.

Deep inside, I had long wanted to escape. I had dreamed of freedom in the quiet moments of my suffering. Yet, when the storm finally came, it wasn't the sense of liberation I had expected. Instead, it was like drowning in a vast sea.

I wish, I could say, I remember those days, but the truth is, I was absent from life itself. The days bled into one another. Time became meaningless. I didn't eat. I barely slept. My thoughts were wild, erratic, circling back to one question: Why wasn't I enough? It's strange how in the midst of wanting out of the marriage, his final rejection felt like my heart being ripped apart.

Through it all, one fragile thought kept me alive: This too shall pass. I whispered it to myself, hoping it would become a truth, a light to cling to, though it often felt more like a lie.

Then came the second envelope,

During the darkest, most desperate hours of my life, when I was too numb to ask for help. My friend, Dr. Kavita Karki, we hadn't been particularly close before. We were more like acquaintances, sharing polite conversations at work and occasionally grabbing tea.

"Hey," she said softly, holding out a small envelope. I blinked in confusion.

"What's this?" I asked, not reaching for it.

"It's nothing big to help," she said, pushing it gently into my hand. I stood there, dumbfounded, as she continued. " I know things haven't been easy for you lately. I just want to do whatever I can. Take it, please."

I opened the envelope, and there it was—a few thousand rupees. I couldn't speak. My throat tightened, and tears blurred my vision. I had never asked her—or anyone—for help. I'd always been too proud, too determined to figure things out on my own. But here she was, offering me the one thing I needed most, without me even asking.

I wanted to argue, to refuse, but the reality of my situation hit me harder than my pride. I felt the dam break, and a tear slid down my cheek.

We didn't speak much after that moment, and when she left, I stood there in the quiet of my small apartment, clutching the envelope. I knew the money would buy me time—time to find my footing, time to breathe. But more than that, Kavita's gesture gave me something even greater: Hope. The kind of hope that reminds you that no matter how dark it gets, there are people who care, even when you least expect it.

From that day onwards, I promised myself I would never forget what it felt like to receive help in my darkest hour. And one day, when the tables turned, I would make sure to be someone else's light in the dark.

I had quietly dropped it off. I hadn't spoken to anyone, hadn't cried for help, but she knew—she just knew.

That was the moment I crumbled. All the pain I had bottled up for years flooded out, and I wept in a way I hadn't allowed myself to earlier. Dr. Karki's quiet presence, the tenderness of her support, saved me. I had thought I was entirely alone, but there she was—offering what I hadn't been able to give myself. No matter how successful I may become, no wealth will ever repay the kindness in that envelope.

I realized that sometimes, in the wreckage of what was once our life, we find the most unexpected saviors.

Topic - 11

Treasures of the Heart: A Celebration of Silent Bonds

"In a world where friendships often seek recognition, there exists a rare and precious bond—the kind that thrives in silence, devoid of accolades or appreciation. These friends don't demand acknowledgment for their unwavering support; they simply show up when the world feels heavy and the path ahead is shrouded in darkness. They are the quiet warriors, standing by your side during your fiercest battles, even when others fade into the background. This profound friendship is a divine gift, one that makes even the heavens envious of the connections forged on Earth.

I have one such friend, Archana. She is not just a brilliant science teacher; she is a beacon of light in my life. From the moment she entered my world, it felt as if she had always belonged. Our connection was inexplicable—a bond woven from the threads of understanding, trust, and unconditional love. When life hurled its most challenging trials at me, when I found myself lost and shelter less, it was Archana who stood by me, a steadfast presence in my darkest hours.

While others turned away, she remained, offering her silent strength like an anchor in a stormy sea. Her support was a gentle whisper of reassurance amidst the chaos, reminding me that I was never truly alone. In those moments of despair, when my spirit was frayed and hope seemed out of reach, Archana embodied the essence of true friendship. She taught me that love doesn't always need to be loud; sometimes, it speaks through quiet gestures, unwavering loyalty, and an open heart.

What I share with Archana goes beyond the ordinary—it is a testament to the kind of friendship that withstands the test of time and trials. She exemplifies what friendship should be: a bond that requires no explanation, no grand gestures, just a profound understanding that transcends words. No one could ever replace her in my heart; her kindness and unwavering support are irreplaceable treasures in my life. Together, we navigate this journey, proving that some friendships are not just relationships—they are lifelines that remind us of our strength, our worth, and the beauty of being truly seen."

The Silent Weight of a Teacher's Life

I agree that teacher shortages can leave students without qualified educators, but there's a moment that haunts me to this day. One of my students, eyes gleaming with excitement, once told me, "I want to be a teacher like you!" She looked at me, waiting for my approval, waiting for that spark of pride or encouragement, hoping for that unspoken connection between a teacher and a student. But all I could offer her was silence—a deep, suffocating silence that spoke of unspoken pain. I wanted to smile, and say the words she longed to hear, but they wouldn't come. My life had never been easy, and the last thing I wanted was for her, or anyone else, to follow the same path. A path lined with heartache, financial strain, and sacrifices unseen by the world.

As the sole earner in my family, I carried the weight of so much more, than just the lesson plans. Every class I taught was another day when I was fighting to keep myself afloat. The pandemic hit us all hard, but for me, it changed everything. When my father passed away, I remember feeling utterly helpless. My brothers had to pool their savings to cover my travel expenses for the funeral. That alone made me feel ashamed, that in such a crucial moment, I wasn't financially capable of doing it on my own. I was drowning in grief, having lost the last man I had to lean on, but that grief had no space to exist in my life.

All I could think about, even as I stood over my father's body, was the financial burden looming over me. Teachers like me don't get the luxury of compassionate leave. We get Casual Leave (CL) at the end of the year, and every day's salary was already budgeted for survival. I had no room for extra expenses. It was all so fragile, like a house of cards on the verge of collapse, and I knew one wrong move would send it all tumbling down.

When I arrived at the funeral, I was already shattered, but seeing my father's lifeless form broke me in ways I hadn't anticipated. The silence in that room was unbearable, like a weight pressing down on my chest, and yet, the noise in my mind was deafening. "How will I survive this?" Who is going to wish me on my birthday saying my, "Gudiya was born today," I kept asking myself. How would I make it without my father's presence, without his advice, without the safety net that I had thought would always be there. My mother was inconsolable, and for the first time in my life, I saw her not as the stern woman I had always known, but as someone broken, lost in her own grief. And I had no space to process my own pain because the next cruel thought that surfaced was: How will I manage without my salary?

The world doesn't stop for our grief. We carry it with us, silently, while going through the motions. I forced myself to keep going, taking online classes through tears because, in this world, survival doesn't wait for anyone. The irony of it all, In the midst of my personal devastation, my coordinator wasn't concerned about my well-being. She was upset that she hadn't been informed that I had rejoined the class after my father's death. Her words still sting. My world had crumbled, and all that mattered was attendance. All that mattered was that the machine kept turning, and my grief was just a pebble caught in its gears.

Years later, history repeated itself. In the middle of a team meeting, my phone rang—my mother had fallen and was in a critical condition. My heart raced as I rushed out, asking for permission. The next day, I returned to work, and no one even asked if I was okay. My mother was holding on to life by a thread in the ICU, waiting, I believe, just for me to see her one last time. Once again, my brothers scrambled to arrange the funds for my travel. I saw her, kissed her forehead, and left the same day. I couldn't afford to stay longer, not with the tuitions, online classes, and my salary that dictated my very survival.

It was February 8th, 24. I was at school, introducing the second language to my PP1 class. I could feel it in my bones—something was wrong. My heart sank as I called my sibling, and the confirmation came: My mother had gone. My world had come crashing down once more. My heart, already so bruised, turned to stone—cold, immovable. My bank account showed single digits, and the burden of paying my daughter's school fees loomed ahead. I had nothing left to give, emotionally or financially.

I stepped outside the classroom for ten minutes to cry, to let out the anguish that had been building inside me for so long. Then I wiped my tears, walked back into that classroom, and continued teaching as if nothing had happened. Only my Hindi family knew the weight I was carrying. That night, I came home, held my online tuitions, and called my siblings to carry on with the funeral arrangements. I couldn't add to their burdens any more than I already had. I couldn't afford to.

Even now, when the world is asleep, and the silence of night creeps in, I whisper, "I'm sorry, Mom. I couldn't make it. I couldn't be there for you."

How could I ever ask one of my students to become a teacher when this is the life I've lived? How could I ask them to carry this silent weight, day after day, with no respite in sight? How could I look them in the eye, knowing the hardships, the sacrifices, the grief that no one sees? This life has given me more pain, than I could ever have imagined. And yet, I continue. But it's not something I wish upon anyone—not even the most eager, bright-eyed student who sees teaching as noble, as fulfilling. It's a burden, I wouldn't wish on another soul.

Personal Reflections

Teaching, like motherhood, is an emotional journey. There are days when I feel drained, when the weight of my students' struggles sits heavy on my shoulders. It's not just about delivering lessons or grading papers; it's about holding space for their emotions, their fears, and their dreams. And sometimes it feels like too much.

I've learned the importance of self-care and of creating boundaries between my role as a teacher and my personal life. Yet, even with those boundaries, it's hard not to carry my students' stories with me. When a student confides in me about their troubles at home, or when I see one of them struggling with anxiety or self-doubt, I feel their pain as if it were my own. But in those moments, I remind myself that being present for them—simply listening and offering kindness—can make a difference, even if I can't solve all their problems.

These sections can expand on the depth of your narrative, showing the intimate connection between teaching and motherhood, and offering personal insights that resonate with universal experiences.

These experiences have reinforced my belief in the importance of emotional intelligence and empathy. I have learned that true success in teaching and parenting comes from understanding and supporting others, not just achieving personal goals.

Hurdles Confronted by Parents and Learners

The Contrast Between Wealth and Emotional Well-Being in Children and Parents.

In today's society, the relationship between wealth and emotional well-being is complex, particularly when examining children and their parents. Financial stability may provide a comfortable lifestyle and access to resources, but it does not guarantee emotional health or happiness. This contrast becomes especially clear when looking at the emotional experiences of children growing up in affluent households, alongside the struggles faced by their parents.

The Burden of Expectations

Children from affluent families often live under the heavy weight of high expectations set by their parents. These expectations may take the form of academic achievement, extracurricular success, or social status. Parents, driven by their own aspirations or sometimes unfulfilled dreams, unknowingly place pressure on their children. As a result, children can feel overwhelmed by the constant demand for perfection, leaving them struggling with anxiety and stress.

Parents' Emotional Struggles

While children navigate the challenges of affluence, parents face their own emotional battles. The pressure to provide the best for their children can create immense stress, leading to long work hours and emotional exhaustion.

This can strain parent-child relationships, as financial concerns take precedence over meaningful engagement.

Affluent parents may also grapple with guilt, questioning whether their wealth is truly benefiting their children or contributing to their emotional difficulties. This guilt can lead to overcompensation, where parents try to buy their children's affection with material goods instead of dedicating time and emotional energy to their upbringing.

The Impact of Material Gifts Over Quality Time in Parenting

In today's fast-paced world, many parents struggle to balance work, personal responsibilities, and family life. As a result, some may turn to material gifts in an attempt to make up for their absence. While these gifts may provide temporary joy, they often fail to build genuine emotional connections or long-term well-being.

Relying on material items instead of quality time can create the illusion of affection. Children may start associating love with possessions, believing that their worth is tied to what they own rather than who they are. This mindset can lead to entitlement and a superficial approach to relationships, eroding the value of deep, meaningful connections.

Growing Children Stop Sharing with Their Parents

As children grow, especially during adolescence, many begin to withdraw from openly communicating with their parents. Several factors contribute to this shift.

1. **Desire for Independence -**

As children enter adolescence, they seek autonomy. They may perceive sharing with parents as a sign of weakness or dependence, making them reluctant to open up.

2. **Influence of Peers -**

During school years, the influence of peers becomes much stronger. Children often prioritize sharing with friends, feeling that their peers better understand their experiences and challenges. The need to fit in and be accepted by friends leads them to confide more in peers than in parents.

3. **Fear of judgment -**

Growing children often worry about how their parents will react to what they share. The fear of being judged, criticized, or misunderstood can create a barrier, discouraging them from expressing their true thoughts and feelings.

4. **Communication Styles -**

The way parents communicate plays a critical role. If parents frequently interrupt, dismiss, or overreact to what their children share, it can create a sense of invalidation. This may cause children to withdraw and stop sharing altogether.

5. **Digital Communication -**

With the rise of technology and social media, many children turn to online platforms for expression. This digital shift often reduces face-to-face interactions with parents, making it easier for them to share thoughts with friends online rather than discussing them with family.

Between Joy and Struggle: A Parent's Dilemma

"Every parent harbors a silent, unspoken wish—a burning desire to give their children the happiness they themselves could never attain. It's an aching need to fill the voids and to rewrite their own story through their child's life. When I found out I was going to be a mother, that yearning was no different. I longed for a daughter, a tiny soul through whom I could relive the dreams I never fully realized. I wanted her to experience the joys I had missed and to be the light that carried forward my hopes.

But the challenge began the moment she found life within me. From the second she existed in my womb, the world around me expected a boy. Society's whispers grew louder, each one carrying the weight of centuries of expectations. I, however, prayed every single moment for a girl. I wanted her with all my heart, not just because I wanted to relive my own life through her, but because I understood the storms she would face. I had endured them. I had battled those same expectations, and I knew—deep within me—that I was the one who could guide her through them, sail her safely through the same tempestuous seas, that I once braved.

This wasn't just about wanting a daughter; this was about preparing to fight for her, to stand strong against a world that would try to tell her who she could or couldn't be. And I was ready."

"The day you become a mother; you are forged into a warrior. The joy that floods your heart is unmatched, a boundless happiness that eclipses anything in this universe. But, as with all great things, this happiness demands a price. From the moment your child is placed in your arms, the battles begin.

Sleepless nights and endless worries—each moment feels like a test of your strength. From cradling them in your arms to watching them grow tall enough to stand shoulder to shoulder with you, you fight through storms of joy, tears, and exhaustion. Every step, every breath, every heartbeat is a war waged between love and struggle, between happiness and hardship. But you press on because there is no turning back. You are a mother—and you are unstoppable."

"No matter how relentless life becomes for you and your children, we must stand unwavering by their side. They will push you away, test your limits, and their defiance will cut deeper than the sharpest labor pains you've endured. But still, you must stand firm. The anguish they inflict may break your spirit, but it's the very burden we must bear.

They are like lost travelers, wandering through a maze of their own making, and yet, we are their compass. Though they stray, they are destined to become the unshakable pillars we stand upon. Leading them is not a choice—it's a duty etched into the fabric of who we are. There is no escape from this path.

Some days will push you to the brink. The weight of their rebellion will suffocate you, and you'll wonder how you can survive being in their presence. But in those moments, remember: your strength is the only thing holding them up. And you will endure."

"Today's parents face a unique set of challenges in raising their children, driven by rapid societal changes, technological advances, and shifting cultural norms. One of the most relatable challenges—one that will make every reader nod in agreement—is the battle with technology and screen time. In a rush of emotion, we often hand our children a 'bomb'—the smartphones, tablets, and computers—and only regret it after each explosion. We struggle to control the time they spend glued to these devices, and we witness the fallout: social media's grip on them, leading to comparison, anxiety, cyberbullying, and a distorted view of the world.

Then, there's the relentless pressure of balancing work and life as we strive to provide them with a better future. But the cost of doing so is taking a toll on us. Time constraints and the rising costs of education—from daycare to college tuition—are putting increasing financial strain on families. We're caught in the grips of a consumerist culture, trying to meet the endless material desires of the modern world. And amidst all this, juggling demanding jobs and family responsibilities leaves us feeling guilty, wondering if we're giving enough of ourselves to our children.

Parental burnout is real. We're constantly pressured to be involved in every aspect of their lives, while somehow maintaining a balance between our personal and professional worlds. The weight of it all is exhausting, and yet, we continue to push forward, hoping we're doing enough."

Future Aspirations

Looking ahead, I aim to continue developing innovative teaching methods and exploring new ways to support my students and children. My goal is to create an environment where everyone can thrive and reach their full potential.

While nurturing a child is vital, finding a balance is key. Educators must teach emotional balance through various methods that emphasize self-awareness, inner peace, and harmony. Encouraging students to develop their own interests and strengths can help them feel more secure in their identities, reducing susceptibility to negative peer pressure.

Here are some key approaches to fostering emotional intelligence and encouraging independence, resilience, and responsibility—qualities essential for facing life's challenges with grace:

1. **Meditation:** Regular meditation practices help students cultivate mindfulness and awareness of their thoughts and feelings, fostering emotional regulation.

2. **Yoga:** Physical postures and breathing exercises harmonize the body and mind, promoting emotional stability and reducing stress.

3. **Promoting Open Communication:** Creating an environment where students feel comfortable discussing their experiences and concerns empowers them to resist unwanted influences.

4. **Philosophical Teachings:** Understanding the interconnectedness of all beings, encourages empathy and compassion. Teaching the value of ethical behavior and personal integrity helps individuals navigate moral dilemmas and make responsible choices. Encouraging exploration of personal values and purpose guides individuals toward fulfilling lives aligned with their passions.

5. **Compassion and Service:** Highlighting the importance of compassion and selfless service fosters a sense of community and social responsibility, inspiring individuals to contribute positively to society. Participation in community service teaches compassion and empathy, grounding emotions in a sense of purpose.

6. **Balance and Harmony:** Teaching the importance of balance in all aspects of life—work, relationships, and self-care—can lead to holistic well-being.

7. **Emotional intelligence:** encouraging awareness and understanding of one's emotions, as well as those of others, enhances communication and relationships.

8. **Reflection and Self-Inquiry:** Students need to engage in self-reflection, examining their emotional responses and understanding their origins.

By integrating these teachings, we can help individuals navigate the complexities of modern life while fostering a sense of connection, purpose, and well-being. Emphasizing resilience encourages individuals to view challenges as opportunities for growth and to develop a mindset that embraces change.

"Beyond Perfection: A Story of Strength and Compassion"

We have commitment to service, and we have to make positive differences in the life of others and in the world around us.

Our understanding of ourselves and our relationship shapes us.

"Don't try to be a god for your children. Let them see that we are all normal human beings, capable of making mistakes. Just as we stand by them when they falter, they should learn to stand by us, too. We aren't perfect, but we are constantly learning and striving to lead a happy life together."

"Parents often feel the pressure to be perfect, to always have the right answers, and to shield their children from mistakes. But true strength lies not in pretending to be infallible, but in showing our children that we are also humans. We make mistakes, we stumble, and we learn. By allowing them to see our vulnerabilities, we teach them a valuable lesson — that life is a continuous journey of growth, not a pursuit of perfection.

When children see that we can acknowledge our mistakes, take responsibility, and learn from them, they learn to do the same. It builds resilience, empathy, and the understanding that everyone, regardless of age, is on a path of self-improvement. Just as we offer patience, guidance, and support when they struggle, they, too, can learn to be compassionate and understanding when we falter.

In embracing our imperfections, we create a nurturing environment where mistakes are seen not as failures but as opportunities for growth. We aren't perfect, but together we are learning, growing, and finding joy in the journey of life. And that's where real happiness lies — not in striving for an impossible standard, but in supporting and learning from one another at every step of the way."

This expanded version adds depth to the original message, focusing on the importance of vulnerability, empathy, and growth.

Topic - 16

Inspirational Elements

As Maya Angelou once said, "We may encounter many defeats, but we must not be defeated." This quote resonates with me deeply and encapsulates my approach to overcoming challenges and persevering through difficulties...

Topic 16: Inspirational Elements:

Individual

Nurturing

Sympathy

Purpose

Independent

Resilience

Attitude

Tenacity

Idealistic

Organized

Novelty

Individual: In a classroom where young minds are blooming, there is a profound difference. Each student is like a unique flower, requiring care and attention to thrive. For a teacher, every individual plays an important role, and engaging with each one is akin to searching for pearls in a deep ocean. To truly connect, you must dive into the students' lives, exploring the emotions they grapple with and the acceptance they yearn for, from us.

It is a daunting job, serving without always being recognized. Yet, the value that an educator builds within their students transcends any measurable scale. It's about nurturing potential, sparking curiosity, and fostering resilience. Addressing their challenges without judgment, a teacher becomes a guiding light, finding creative ways to enlighten those little souls.

Each day brings new stories, hidden struggles, and moments of joy. A simple smile or a word of encouragement can change a student's trajectory, revealing their inner strengths and capabilities. The classroom transforms into a sanctuary, where students feel safe to express themselves, to take risks, and to explore their passions.

As educators, we often carry the weight of our students' dreams and fears. We become advocates for their voices, champions of their aspirations, and allies in their journey toward self-discovery. The bonds we create can last a lifetime, influencing not only academic achievements but also the very essence of who they become as individuals.

In this intricate dance of teaching and learning, we learn just as much from our students as they do from us. Their laughter, their struggles, and their triumphs enrich our lives, reminding us of the beauty and complexity of the human experience. Ultimately, teaching is not just about imparting knowledge; it's about nurturing hearts and minds, one precious pearl at a time.

Nurturing: Nurturing Young Minds is a beautiful concept that encompasses the process of fostering growth, curiosity, and emotional well-being in children. It involves creating a supportive environment where young learners feel safe to explore, ask questions, and develop their unique identities.

A crucial aspect of this nurturing process is emotional support. Providing a safe space for children to express their feelings and thoughts is essential for helping them build confidence and resilience. When children know they can share their emotions without fear of judgment, they are more likely to engage authentically with their learning journey.

To foster lifelong learning, we must encourage curiosity. This means stimulating a love for learning by inviting questions and promoting exploration. Allowing children to discover their interests and passions can ignite their desire to learn, leading them to seek knowledge beyond what is taught in the classroom. Engaging in hands-on activities, interactive discussions, and creative projects can make learning exciting and relevant.

Recognizing that each child learns differently is vital. Adapting teaching methods to meet their specific needs not only fosters their strengths but also addresses challenges they may face. This personalized approach helps to create a more inclusive classroom where every child feels valued and understood.

Building strong relationships with students is equally important. Establishing trust and connection enhances their learning experience and creates a sense of belonging. When children feel that their teachers genuinely care about them, they are more likely to participate actively and take risks in their learning. This relationship also provides a foundation for effective communication, allowing children to express their thoughts and concerns openly.

Additionally, involving families in the nurturing process strengthens the support network for each child. Encouraging parental engagement in their child's education fosters a holistic approach to learning, reinforcing the values and skills being developed in the classroom.

By nurturing young minds, we can help shape the next generation, equipping them with the tools they need to thrive academically and personally. The impact of this nurturing can extend far beyond school, influencing their relationships, career paths, and contributions to society. Ultimately, by fostering a love for learning, emotional intelligence, and strong interpersonal skills, we empower children to become compassionate, confident, and capable adults who will positively impact the world around them.

Sympathy: "Teaching sympathy and modeling it for students is crucial for today's generation. When teachers demonstrate sympathy, they create a safe and nurturing environment where students feel understood and valued. This emotional support helps students cope with both academic and personal challenges, fostering their overall well-being.

Sympathy also builds trust between teachers and students. When students feel that their teachers genuinely care about their feelings and experiences, they are more likely to engage and participate in the learning process. Teaching students' sympathy encourages the development of empathy for others, as these two elements are interconnected and essential. Together, they foster a compassionate classroom environment, reducing bullying and promoting positive relationships.

Sympathy and empathy are vital components of effective communication and social interaction. When students learn these skills, they are better equipped to navigate social situations, resolve conflicts, and collaborate with others. A sympathetic approach also promotes inclusivity by recognizing and respecting diverse backgrounds and experiences, which helps create a sense of belonging for all students.

When students feel emotionally supported, they are more likely to take academic risks, ask questions, and seek help when needed, leading to improved academic performance and a greater love for learning. Additionally, being sympathetic not only helps students support their peers but also strengthens their own emotional resilience. Understanding others' feelings provides them with the tools to manage their emotions and challenges more effectively.

A classroom culture rooted in sympathy encourages positive behavior among students. When sympathy is both modeled and taught, it reduces negative behaviors and fosters kindness and cooperation."

Purpose: Purpose is the reason or intention behind actions, thoughts, or existence. It gives direction, motivation, and meaning to what we do or experience. For individuals, purpose helps guide decisions, offers a sense of fulfillment, and provides a sense of belonging or meaning in life.

A teacher plays a crucial role in helping a child discover and understand their purpose by nurturing their talents, interests, and values. Teachers create opportunities for students to reflect on their interests, strengths, and goals. Through activities like journaling, discussions, and project-based learning, students begin to understand what excites and motivates them.

By guiding students to think critically about the world and their role in it, teachers help them form a deeper sense of purpose. Teachers can challenge students to ask questions like, *"What do I want to contribute to the world?"* or *"What kind of person do I want to become?"*

Teachers often act as mentors, offering personal guidance that inspires a student's sense of direction. By sharing their own experiences, teachers model how to live with purpose and provide advice as students explore their own paths.

Teaching students the importance of setting and working towards goals also gives them a sense of purpose. By helping them set realistic, meaningful, and personal goals, teachers show students that purpose is not something fixed, but something they can shape over time.

Perhaps most importantly, teachers inspire a sense of purpose by encouraging students to think about how they can make a positive impact on others. Projects that involve community service, leadership roles, or helping peers allow students to connect their personal purpose to a larger societal goal.

Independent: "Encouraging a child to take ownership of their own learning fosters independence and prepares them for life. By giving students choices in what and how they learn, teachers help them take control of their educational journey. This might involve offering different options for projects, allowing self-paced learning, or letting students set personal academic goals. These strategies foster responsibility and self-motivation.

Teachers can promote independent thinking by asking open-ended questions and encouraging students to analyze, evaluate, and come up with their own solutions. This develops problem-solving skills, helping students rely on their reasoning rather than waiting for answers.

Teachers also play a role in teaching practical life skills like time management, goal setting, and decision-making. These skills are essential for students to navigate both their academic and personal lives independently. Allowing students to experience failure and learn from it is key to fostering independence. Teachers can create a classroom environment where mistakes are seen as learning opportunities rather than setbacks, which builds resilience and confidence in students to try again.

Regularly encouraging students to reflect on their learning, behavior, and progress helps them become more self-aware. This reflection promotes independent growth as students begin to understand their strengths and areas for improvement, allowing them to take responsibility for their actions and choices.

Instead of giving direct answers, teachers can guide students through the process of discovery. By asking guiding questions or suggesting resources, teachers help students learn how to find answers on their own, promoting independence in their learning.

A teacher's encouragement and positive reinforcement help build a child's self-esteem. When students feel confident in their abilities, they are more likely to take initiative and work independently. Teachers can also push students to step out of their comfort zones, further strengthening their independence.

While independence involves individual responsibility, learning to work with others is also essential. Teachers can encourage students to collaborate, lead, and problem-solve in group settings. This promotes independent thinking within a team context, preparing students for real-life situations where they'll need to be both self-reliant and cooperative.

Resilience: Building resilience in students is a crucial part of a teacher's role, helping them develop the ability to overcome challenges, adapt to change, and bounce back from setbacks. A positive, nurturing classroom environment is the foundation for resilience. When students feel safe, supported, and respected, they are more likely to take risks and face challenges without fear of judgment. Teachers can foster this by promoting a culture of respect, empathy, and open communication.

Encouraging students to approach problems with a solution-focused mindset builds resilience. Teachers can present real-life scenarios or challenges and guide students through the process of identifying the problem, brainstorming solutions, and taking action. This equips students with the skills they need to navigate obstacles.

Failure is an inevitable part of life, but many students fear it. Teachers can help students reframe failure as an opportunity for growth. By discussing famous figures who failed before succeeding, or sharing their own experiences, teachers can show that setbacks are part of the learning process. Offering constructive feedback and focusing on effort rather than just results reinforces this mindset.

A growth mindset—the belief that abilities and intelligence can be developed through effort and learning—is closely tied to resilience. Teachers can foster this by praising perseverance, effort, and improvement, rather than innate ability. They can encourage students to embrace challenges and view them as opportunities to grow rather than as insurmountable obstacles.

Resilience also involves managing emotions effectively. Teachers can teach students strategies to handle stress, disappointment, or frustration. Techniques like mindfulness, breathing exercises, or journaling can help students stay calm and grounded during difficult times. Developing emotional intelligence allows students to navigate their emotions in healthy ways.

Giving students opportunities to make decisions, take on responsibilities, and learn from their actions fosters independence and resilience. When students are trusted to manage tasks and experience the consequences (both positive and negative) of their choices, they learn accountability and adaptability.

Teachers serve as role models. By sharing their own experiences of overcoming challenges or setbacks, teachers can demonstrate resilience in action. Modeling calm and perseverance in difficult situations shows students how to approach adversity in a constructive way.

Helping students set realistic goals and break them down into manageable steps builds confidence and resilience. Achieving small successes along the way motivates students to keep going, even when things get tough. Teachers can guide students in setting goals and tracking their progress.

Resilient individuals often have a strong support network. Teachers can promote teamwork, peer support, and positive relationships in the classroom. Encouraging collaboration, active listening, and empathy helps students build a community of support they can rely on during challenging times.

Resilience is about adapting to changing circumstances. Teachers can prepare students for this by promoting flexibility in learning and problem-solving. Encourage students to try different approaches and adapt their strategies when things don't go as planned helps them develop the ability to adjust in the face of adversity.

Recognizing students' effort, perseverance, and small victories—even when the final outcome isn't perfect—reinforces resilience. Celebrating progress encourages students to keep trying, even when they face difficulties, knowing their efforts are valued.

Attitude: Setting up the right attitude in life is essential because it serves as the foundation for how we perceive and respond to the world around us. A positive attitude allows us to view challenges, as opportunities for growth rather than obstacles, shaping our mindset and making us more resilient in the face of adversity.

Our attitude also significantly impacts our interactions with others. A kind, open-minded, and understanding attitude fosters better relationships, building trust, cooperation, and respect. Positivity is contagious; when you radiate it, you inspire those around you to adopt a similar mindset, creating a supportive and uplifting environment for everyone.

A proactive attitude encourages self-reflection and learning from experiences. It enables us to embrace change, adapt to new situations, and continuously improve ourselves. In essence, the right attitude serves as a compass, guiding decisions, shaping life experiences, and influencing overall happiness and success.

Teachers play a crucial role in shaping students' attitudes, not just toward learning but toward life. By helping students witness challenges as opportunities for growth, teachers reinforce the idea that intelligence and abilities can be developed through effort and persistence. Praising hard work, rather than just the outcomes, helps students focus on the learning process rather than solely on results.

Recognizing and celebrating students' efforts—no matter how small—provides positive reinforcement. Through praise, awards, and constructive feedback, teachers motivate students to keep trying, fostering a sense of accomplishment and self-worth. Creating a classroom atmosphere where students feel safe to express themselves and take risks—without fear of judgment—promotes confidence and allows for the exploration of new challenges.

Teachers also serve as role models. By demonstrating optimism, patience, and a can-do attitude, they inspire students to adopt similar behaviors. Showing students how to handle setbacks gracefully teaches them that maintaining a positive attitude leads to better outcomes.

Another key factor in shaping attitudes is helping students recognize and manage their emotions. By fostering emotional intelligence—encouraging empathy, self-regulation, and social skills—teachers guide students toward navigating difficult situations with a positive outlook. Setting achievable academic and personal goals further contributes to this growth; when students experience success, even in small milestones, their confidence grows, promoting a positive attitude toward future challenges.

Making learning enjoyable is essential. Incorporating interactive activities, creativity, and humor into lessons helps students associate learning with fun and engagement, leading to a more positive attitude toward school.

Encouraging self-reflection is vital as well. By assisting students in reflecting on their experiences and progress, teachers help them identify areas for improvement and acknowledge their growth. This process fosters self-awareness and motivates students to adopt a positive, forward-thinking attitude. When students understand that failure is a stepping stone to success, they are less likely to fear mistakes and more inclined to maintain a positive attitude in the face of challenges. Providing opportunities for leadership and responsibility within the classroom builds confidence and fosters a sense of ownership and pride, further contributing to a positive attitude.

Tenacity: Tenacity is a crucial trait for students, as it empowers them to navigate challenges and setbacks throughout their academic journey. Schoolwork often involves demanding subjects, tough exams, and overwhelming projects. Rather than giving up when the workload intensifies, tenacity helps students persist and overcome obstacles. This ability to bounce back from failure is a key life skill, and it cultivates resilience, teaching students how to handle disappointment and keep moving forward.

Academic success often requires sustained effort over time. Whether it's striving for good grades, completing a degree, or mastering a particular skill, tenacity helps students stay focused on their long-term goals. By persevering through difficulties, students not only advance academically but also improve their problem-solving abilities. Tenacious students learn to think creatively, finding new approaches to tackle difficult tasks instead of abandoning them at their first difficulty.

Furthermore, tenacity fosters self-discipline, which is essential for managing time, maintaining focus, and meeting deadlines. This is particularly important when balancing academic responsibilities with extracurricular activities and personal life. As students push through obstacles and achieve success, they build confidence in their abilities. This growing self-assurance motivates them to take on even greater challenges in the future.

Building tenacity in students is a gradual process that requires fostering a growth mindset, resilience, and perseverance. By helping students cultivate these traits, we can support them in becoming not only academically successful but also more capable of overcoming challenges in life.

Idealistic: Idealism plays a pivotal role in students' lives, influencing not only their academic performance but also their personal development. By providing a sense of purpose and direction, idealism helps guide students' actions and decisions, leading them toward positive growth.

Being idealistic can benefit students in many ways, particularly by inspiring them with a strong sense of purpose and a drive for positive change. Idealistic students often have clear visions of how things should be, which fuels their motivation. They aim high and work diligently toward their ideals, whether that means making a difference in their community, excelling academically, or improving their personal skills. This sense of purpose becomes a powerful force that drives their academic efforts.

Idealists also tend to think outside the box. They are not limited by traditional thinking or perceived barriers, encouraging creative problem-solving. For students, this can translate to approaching assignments, projects, and challenges in unique and innovative ways, allowing them to stand out.

Idealism often involves holding on to a vision despite obstacles. For students, this leads to greater perseverance and a refusal to give up when challenges arise. They continue pushing toward their goals, fueled by the belief that they can create the future they envision.

A strong sense of ethics frequently guides idealistic students. Their desire to do what's right helps them make responsible decisions both academically and personally. This commitment to integrity fosters positive actions that benefit not only themselves but also those around them.

Idealism can also inspire leadership in students. Those who believe in making the world a better place often take the initiative to lead and influence their peers toward positive change. This may involve leading student groups, initiating impactful projects, or simply being a role model for others.

While idealists can sometimes be seen as overly optimistic, their outlook actually helps them remain hopeful, even during tough times. Rather than being discouraged by setbacks, they stay focused on the bigger picture, confident that improvement and success are always possible.

In summary, idealism helps students aim for higher standards, think creatively, act ethically, and persevere through challenges. These qualities not only contribute to their academic growth but also shape their character, preparing them for future success.

Organized: Being organized is essential in a student's life for several reasons, as it directly impacts their academic performance, personal growth, and overall well-being. Organization helps students manage their time effectively. By keeping track of assignments, deadlines, and study schedules, students can allocate time efficiently, avoiding last-minute cramming or rushing through work. This ensures they stay on top of their responsibilities without feeling overwhelmed.

When students are organized, they can focus better and work more efficiently. An organized workspace and structured study plan reduce distractions and help them concentrate on what's important. This leads to higher productivity, enabling them to complete tasks in less time. On the other hand, a lack of organization can lead to missed deadlines, incomplete work, and unnecessary last-minute stress. Being organized allows students to stay in control of their academic and personal tasks, reducing anxiety and preventing feelings of being overwhelmed.

Organization directly contributes to better academic outcomes. By planning ahead, keeping notes in order, and reviewing materials regularly, students are better prepared for exams, projects, and presentations. This systematic approach often leads to higher grades and a deeper understanding of the subjects they study. Organized students tend to be more disciplined because they set priorities and follow their plans. This focus helps them avoid procrastination and distractions, common barriers to success in school.

Staying organized also ensures that students can meet both academic and extracurricular deadlines. By using a calendar or planner, students are able to manage multiple responsibilities—such as homework, exams, sports and social activities—without missing important deadlines or feeling overwhelmed.

Moreover, organization is a valuable life skill that extends beyond school. Learning to stay organized during their academic years helps students develop habits that will benefit them in both their personal and professional lives in the future. When students are organized, they are more likely to complete tasks on time and stay ahead of their work. This boosts their confidence and provides a sense of accomplishment, motivating them to maintain good habits and remain proactive.

Novelty: Novelty plays an important role in a student's life, contributing to both academic success and personal development. New experiences and ideas stimulate curiosity, encourage creativity, and help students engage more deeply with learning. Novelty sparks curiosity, which is crucial for intellectual growth. When students are exposed to new concepts, approaches, or subjects, their natural curiosity is engaged, making them more interested in learning and exploring topics in greater depth.

Encountering novel ideas and experiences encourages students to think outside the box. Novelty challenges their thinking, prompting them to explore different perspectives and come up with creative solutions—especially beneficial in problem-solving and project-based learning. Routine can sometimes lead to boredom, causing students to disengage from their studies. Novelty breaks this monotony, helping reigniting their interest in learning. When students are introduced to new teaching methods, fresh challenges, or exciting materials, they are more likely to stay motivated and focused.

Exposure to new situations or experiences also helps students become more adaptable. Novelty teaches them how to handle unfamiliar challenges, which is a vital life skill. It builds resilience and equips students to thrive in dynamic environments, both inside and outside the classroom.

Novelty often challenges students to step out of their comfort zones and embrace new opportunities. This fosters a growth mindset, where students view challenges as opportunities for learning and growth rather than obstacles to avoid. It promotes lifelong learning and a willingness to take on difficult tasks.

Experiencing novelty also helps students discover new interests, passions, and talents. It encourages them to try new activities, meet different people, and explore unfamiliar areas of knowledge. This personal growth contributes to building self-confidence and shaping a sense of identity.

In summary, novelty is essential in a student's life because it stimulates curiosity, enhances creativity, and boosts engagement. It helps students develop adaptability, improve memory retention, and foster a growth mindset, all of which is vital for both academic and personal success.

IMP: Reader Engagement:

I invite you to reflect on your own experiences as educators and parents. What challenges have you faced, and how have you overcome them? Consider how you can apply these insights to enhance your own practices and make a positive impact.

www.ingramcontent.com/pod-product-compliance
Lightning Source LLC
LaVergne TN
LVHW061552070526
838199LV00077B/7016